CLASSIC

ONE-LINERS

Gene Perret
Bob Hope's Head Comedy Writer

with Terry Perret Martin

ILLUSTRATED BY MYRON MILLER

Happy New Year Joe & ___!

Sterling Publishing Co., Inc.
New York

Edited by Jeanette Green

Library of Congress Cataloging-in-Publication Data

Perret, Gene.
　Classic one-liners / by Gene Perret & Terry Perret Martin ;
illustrated by Myron Miller.
　　　p.　　cm.
　　ISBN 0-8069-0722-3
　　1. Wit and humor, Juvenile. I. Martin, Terry Perret. II. Title.
PN6163.P456　1994
818'.5402—dc20

94-28144
CIP
AC

1　3　5　7　9　10　8　6　4　2

Published by Sterling Publishing Company, Inc.
387 Park Avenue South, New York, N.Y. 10016
© 1994 by Gene Perret & Terry Perret Martin
Distributed in Canada by Sterling Publishing
% Canadian Manda Group, One Atlantic Avenue, Suite 105
Toronto, Ontario, Canada M6K 3E7
Distributed in Great Britain and Europe by Cassell PLC
Villiers House, 41/47 Strand, London WC2N 5JE, England
Distributed in Australia by Capricorn Link (Australia) Pty Ltd.
P.O. Box 6651, Baulkham Hills, Business Centre, NSW 2153,
Australia
Manufactured in the United States of America
All rights reserved

Sterling ISBN 0-8069-0722-3

CONTENTS

INTRODUCTION

All of us love a bargain. It's thrilling to get a good value at an inexpensive price. We're not necessarily being cheap or penny-pinching; we simply want to get the most for our effort.

There's an economy of words that we appreciate, too. We like writing that is compact, concise, that packs a wealth of meaning into a few well-selected, accurate, effective words. Many competent essayists could write paragraphs and pages about apprehension and hesitation caused by it, yet not say as much about the subject as Shakespeare did: "Doubts are traitors and make us lose the good we oft might win by fearing to attempt."

Wisdom is most powerful and clear when it's expressed in an economy of words.

One-liners are a double bargain. They pack a powerful one-two punch of wit and wisdom into a short sentence or two. They not only say something, but say it in a funny, potent, and memorable way.

Mark Twain said, "When I was a boy of fourteen, my father was so ignorant I could hardly stand to have the old man around. But when I got to be twenty-one, I was astonished at how much he had learned in seven years."

That statement speaks worlds not only about Twain and his dad, but about all dads and all sons. It's a short treatise on adolescence and maturity.

When asked about his political affiliation, Will Rogers said, "I belong to no organized political party. I'm a Democrat." That amuses us and tells us quite a bit about Rogers, the Democrats, and politics.

Those are memorable one-liners. They've survived for a number of years. They're truly classics.

That's what this book is—a collection of classic one-liners about many different topics. They're funny lines that capture an abundance of wit and wisdom in a few carefully selected words.

5

"There is no such thing as fun for the entire family."
—*Jerry Seinfeld*

If you watch a game, it's fun. If you play at it, it's recreation. If you work at it, it's golf. —*Bob Hope*

Want to have some fun? Walk into an antique shop and say, "What's new?" —*Henny Youngman*

Want to have some fun? Send someone a telegram and on top put "page 2." —*Henny Youngman*

Want to have some fun? Send someone a telegram saying, "Ignore first telegram." —*Henny Youngman*

Good women are no fun. The only good woman I can recall was Betsy Ross and all she ever made was a flag. —*Mae West*

Did you ever hear someone say this: "It was more fun than a barrel of monkeys." Did you ever *smell* a barrel of monkeys? —*Steve Bluestein*

★ ★ ★ ★ ★

Always try to keep a smile on your face because it looks silly on other parts of your body.

I used to proclaim that "laughter is the best medicine" until my family doctor sued me for practicing without a license.

—— ★ ——

Let a smile be your umbrella and see if you don't get a lot of strange looks during the next thunder shower.

We should have a lot of big belly laughs tonight because this audience is certainly equipped for it.

Smile even when you're unhappy because there's a good chance it'll make the people who are happier than you a little less happy.

It's easy for everyone to have at least one good belly laugh a day. All you need is a full length mirror in the same room where you take your shower.

I adopted the philosophy of life: "If it ain't fun, don't do it." The first person to lose money because of it was my dentist.

Try to keep a smile on your face and a melody in your heart. Once you master that, try patting your head and rubbing your belly at the same time.

Remember that "laughter" spelled backwards is "rethgual." It means absolutely nothing, but it just might cheer you up.

You show me a man who can't take a joke and I'll show you a man who should never wear Bermuda shorts in public.

I love to hear laughter from an audience because sometimes *I* don't know where the punch lines are.

One speaker told us a funny joke he heard. It was funny when he heard it, but not when he told it.

———— ★ ————

GAMES

I never got respect. I remember when I was a kid and played hide and seek . . . they wouldn't even look for me.
—*Rodney Dangerfield*

I stayed up one night playing poker with Tarot cards. I got a full house and four people died. —*Steven Wright*

I bet on a horse ten-to-one. It didn't come in until half past five. —*Henny Youngman*

No horse can go as fast as the money you bet on him.
—*Nate Collier*

Race track: A place where windows clean people.
—*Henny Youngman*

The horse I bet on was so late getting home, he tiptoed into the stable. —*Henny Youngman*

Never play peek-a-boo with a child on a long plane trip. There's no end to the game. Finally I grabbed him by the bib and said, "Look. It's always gonna be me."
—*Rita Rudner*

The only game I like to play is Old Maid—provided she's not too old. —*Groucho Marx*

They love their gambling in Atlantic City. I saw a guy putting a quarter in the parking meter. I said, "Are you crazy?" He said, "Look at the odds—8 to 5." —*Bob Hope*

9

My horse finished so far back, the jockey had to run ahead
of him with a flashlight.   —*Bob Hope*

I follow the horses. And the horses I follow, follow horses.
                                             —*Joe E. Lewis*

★   ★   ★   ★   ★

Gambling . . . that's throwing money away while other people cheer you on.

—— ★ ——

Casino gambling is strange. You put down five dollars,
they spin the wheel, take your money, and tell you what a
good time you're having.

—— ★ ——

My brother was real good at playing hide-and-seek. He
was so good at it, we haven't seen him since 1952.

—— ★ ——

I didn't like to play hide-and-seek when I was young. My
invisible playmate always won.

—— ★ ——

I never liked hide-and-seek. Not since the time I hid in the
closet and my family moved.

—— ★ ——

I was never very good at sports. When I played in Little
League, my own father traded me to another team.

. . . for ten dollars and a child to be born later.

—— ★ ——

When I played in choose-up baseball games, they'd tell me
to stand out in right field. Then the two teams would go
play on another field.

—— ★ ——

When I played football, I was known as "Crazy Legs" until
I was 12 years old. That's when I learned to put my pants
on with the zipper in front.

—— ★ ——

We used to play spin-the-bottle when I was a kid. A girl would spin the bottle, and if the bottle pointed to you when it stopped, the girl could either kiss you or give you a nickel. By the time I was 14, I owned my own home.

—— ★ ——

My best game as a kid was tiddlywinks until I had a career-ending injury.

. . . I sprained my wink finger.

It could have been worse. I could have broken my tiddly.

—— ★ ——

My friend thought he was not gonna make it, then he started thinking positive. Now he's positive he's not gonna make it. —*Sammy Shore*

It's hard to be nice to some paranoid schizophrenic just because she lives in your body. —*Judy Tenuta*

Right now I'm having amnesia and déjà vu at the same time. —*Steven Wright*

Psychiatry is when you spend $50 an hour to squeal on yourself. —*Harry Hershfield*

One psychiatrist I know used shock treatment. He gives you the bill in advance. —*Harry Hershfield*

11

My boyfriend and I broke up. He wanted to get married and I didn't want him to.
—*Rita Rudner*

I quit therapy because my analyst was trying to help me behind my back.
—*Richard Lewis*

I'm getting fed up with my psychiatrist. I told him I had suicidal tendencies. From now on I have to pay in advance.
—*Rodney Dangerfield*

People today say they've got to "find themselves." My mother would have said to them, "If you'd put things away when you're done with them . . . ."

If I ever told my father, "I'm trying to get my head on straight," he would have knocked it off for me.

A lot of people today play "head games," but I don't. I don't want to buy a lot of expensive equipment.

I tried to make an appointment with my shrink, but he couldn't take me. He was having a visit with his shrink.

I asked my shrink to show me one positive result from all my visits. He showed me his new Porsche.

Everybody is looking for equality today. They all want more of it than the next guy.

Greed is one of the seven deadly sins. I know a guy who's so greedy he has eight deadly sins.

. . . He had one custom made.

Greed is silly. You come into this world with nothing and you leave with nothing. Except when you leave, you have to pay taxes on it.

—— ★ ——

Diogenes searched the world over and could not find ten honest men—and that was before politics became an art form.

—— ★ ——

I believe in honesty and integrity. Someone asked me what I would do if I found $1 million in the street. If it belonged to a poor person, I'd give it back.

—— ★ ——

Today everyone wants instant gratification no matter how long it takes.

—— ★ ——

I knew I was an unwanted baby when I saw that my bath toys were a toaster and a radio.   —*Joan Rivers*

My parents put a live teddy bear in my crib.
                              —*Woody Allen*

To show you how wild my kids are, my eight-year-old bought a bicycle with the money he saved by not smoking.
                              —*Phyllis Diller*

We had a quicksand box in our backyard. I was an only child, eventually.   —*Steven Wright*

★   ★   ★   ★   ★

Men never outgrow their love of childhood toys. Many of them never outgrow childhood.

—— ★ ——

You show me a child who doesn't play with toys and I'll show you a father who's not done with them yet.

—— ★ ——

I bought my son a toy that was absolutely guaranteed to be completely unbreakable. He used it to break all his other toys.

—— ★ ——

Some new toys are so complicated that *only* a child can operate them.

—— ★ ——

Kids only want high technology toys nowadays. My son has an imaginary playmate that requires batteries.

—— ★ ——

Toys are getting more and more expensive and complicated. I saw one that was $29.95—for the instruction booklet.

—— ★ ——

There should be a law: anything that costs over $49.95 should not be labeled a plaything.

—— ★ ——

I saw one toy that was labeled accurately. It said, "recommended for children ages 6 to 12 provided they can get their hands on $46.50."

—— ★ ——

Why is it that the more expensive a toy is, the more inclined the child is to play with the box it came in?

—— ★ ——

When I see the words "some assembly required" written on the side of a box, I always feel they should have after them "by a better man than me."

—— ★ ——

I knew a guy who once bought a defective boomerang. He couldn't return it.

—— ★ ——

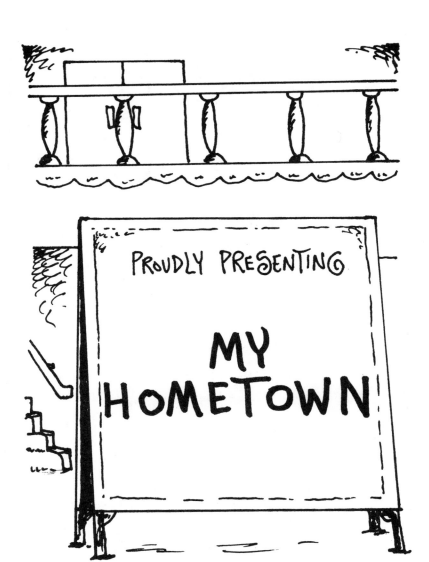

"It was hard for me to leave my hometown
. . . covered in tar and feathers as I was."
—*Gene Perret*

This town was so small they had a fashion show at Sears. No models, they just held open the catalog and the women would point.
—*Joan Rivers*

This is a small town. Their 7–Eleven is called 2–Five.
—*Joan Rivers*

His hometown is so small, the road map is actual size.
—*Milton Berle*

This town was so small, the all-night drugstore closed at noon.
—*Jackie Vernon*

I once played in a town so small that if you went out for a night on the town, it took only half an hour.
—*Jack E. Leonard*

I hate small towns because once you've seen the cannon in the park, there's nothing else to do.
—*Lenny Bruce*

★ ★ ★ ★ ★

Our town was so small it only had two streets in it—Main Street and Non-Main Street

Our town was so small, to make it look bigger, we put a mirror at one end of it.

Ours used to be a one-horse town, until the horse quit.

—— ★ ——

Our town was so small that we had to close the public library. Someone tore a few pages out of the book.

—— ★ ——

Everything was small in our town. Even our sheriff only had room for three points on his badge.

—— ★ ——

This town was so small, if you sneezed, everybody in town said, "God bless you."

—— ★ ——

Our town was so small, if two people stopped to talk, it was considered a town meeting.

—— ★ ——

Our town was so small the mayor also had to double as the village idiot.

. . . He did well in both positions

—— ★ ——

All the towns were small where I lived. At our Little League ball park, each base was in a different county.

—— ★ ——

The big excitement in my town was to go down to the railroad station and watch them give haircuts.

—*Herb Shriner*

A dull town is one in which there's no place to go where
you shouldn't be.   —*Alexander Woollcott*

His hometown is so dull the drugstore sells picture post-
cards of other towns.   —*Milton Berle*

The only way to have fun in his hometown is to move
away.   —*Milton Berle*

Our town is so dull that at the annual Fourth of July picnic, we had a firework.

The leader of our local biker club rides a moped.

Our town is so dull that our local newspaper doesn't even
have a front page.

In our post office they put up wanted posters of all the
people who have books overdue at the library.

Our town is so dull we had one resident who was in a coma
for three months. He woke up, and hadn't missed a thing.

The most excitement our town had was the heated debate
over installing a traffic light on Main Street. It wasn't
whether to install it or not; it was over what color the lights
should be.

We only have two traffic signs in our town. The first one
says "Stop." The second says "Stop What?"

Even though our town has very little crime, we still have a
very efficient police force—except when he's not feeling
well.

Nothing ever happens in our town. Our town gossip had to hire a writing staff.

—— ★ ——

Ours is a quiet little town. In fact, one resident sued his next-door neighbor because he claimed his grass was growing too loud.

—— ★ ——

The high school football games draw about 500 people on Friday evenings. They draw a little bit more if the other team shows up.

—— ★ ——

The biggest spectacle is when someone is going to board the train to leave town. You see, our town doesn't have a train stop.

—— ★ ——

He's just the candidate to get our town moving. I know if he wins, I'm moving.   —*Milton Berle*

Our town elected a new police chief. His first job was to arrest the old police chief.   —*Milton Berle*

The only way to combat criminals is by not voting for them.   —*Dayton Allen*

★   ★   ★   ★   ★

Our town had the crookedest mayor in history. Even the sign in City Hall that directed you to the mayor's office said, "Go down this corridor and under the table."

Yes, the mayor was so crooked, he had his office under a table.

. . . He wanted to be near his money.

Our mayor took all kinds of bribes. When he raised his right hand to take the oath of office, somebody put money in it.

He lived off graft. He was the only mayor I ever saw whose office had an opening in the door for night deposits.

His campaign slogan was: "It's your money. Why give it to a stranger?"

In his office at City Hall, he had the first dollar he ever made framed and hanging on the wall . . . along with the brown paper bag it came in.

This politician had his hand out so often his palm was sunburned.

But you always knew where to find the mayor. He was always either in his office or in somebody else's pocket.

He loved money. When they played the National Anthem, he'd put his hands over his wallet.

He would be away from his office for long stretches of time, too. Sometimes 3 to 5 years.

He was a crooked politician. To open the Little League each season, instead of throwing out the first ball, he would steal the first base.

. . . and he'd keep it.

—— ★ ——

Gossip is when you hear something you like about someone you don't.
                                                    —*Earl Wilson*

What a talker he is. He could persuade a fish to come out and take a walk with him.   —*Mark Twain*

My wife says she doesn't like to repeat gossip, but she says, "What else is there to do with it?"   —*Milton Berle*

You can't believe everything you hear, but it's fun to repeat it anyway.   —*Milton Berle*

★   ★   ★   ★   ★

People loved to spread gossip in our town. It got so bad the telephone company had to install speed bumps on all the party lines.

—— ★ ——

Every town has gossip. If you don't hear any, you're it.

—— ★ ——

Our town had such hot gossip going back and forth over the back fence, that sometimes the fence would catch fire.

—— ★ ——

One lady in our town spent so much time spreading gossip over the back fence, that her tongue had splinters.

—— ★ ——

We had one lady in town who could spread gossip so fast, they had to paint a racing stripe down her tongue.

—— ★ ——

This lady was lightning quick and ferocious at spreading rumors. She had a black belt in the English language.

—— ★ ——

Often she could tell the entire neighborhood what you did before you were done doing it.

—— ★ ——

This lady tried very hard to keep a secret. In fact, she'd always get ten or twelve people to help her keep it.

—— ★ ——

She never stopped spreading gossip. Even when she was asleep, the teeth in the glass by her bedside would continue to talk about people.

—— ★ ——

She was a very mean gossip. She'd go around spreading the truth behind people's backs.

—— ★ ——

Her philosophy was: if she didn't have anything good to say about a person, she'd say it anyway.

—— ★ ——

Of course, really juicy gossip is something you wouldn't believe in a million years, but it sure is fun hearing it.

—— ★ ——

Start every day off with a smile and get it over with.
—*W. C. Fields*

This neighbor is a real grouch. If she were an island, she'd fight with the water.
—*Bob Hope*

★　　★　　★　　★　　★

Our town had the grouchiest neighbor in the world. In front of her door she had a man-eating welcome mat.

This lady was a real grouch. She had the personality of World War II.

This lady was so grouchy, when she came out to pick up her milk in the morning, it would curdle.

Nobody liked her. Even the paperboy wouldn't go near her house. He'd call her on the phone and read the news to her.

She was such a mean old lady, the local dentist would charge her extra. Apparently, fangs are a lot more difficult to work on.

She was so mean, she didn't like anything that was fun. The dentist even found out she was allergic to laughing gas.

. . . He had to give her snarling gas.

—— ★ ——

This lady was always frowning. Anytime she wanted to smile, she had to get two friends to help her.

—— ★ ——

She was mean. When she chased kids away from her house, everyone ran. Even the snails left skid marks.

—— ★ ——

Even the ASPCA had an injunction against her. She was scaring all the pit bulls in the neighborhood.

—— ★ ——

When the welcome wagon came to her door she shot at it.

—— ★ ——

This lady was so bad that her dog put up a sign on her lawn that said, "Beware of My Master."

—— ★ ——

The guy who invented the first wheel was an idiot. The guy who invented the other three . . . he was a genius.
—*Sid Caesar*

Our village idiot locked his keys in the car. It took him an hour and a half to get his wife out. —*Henny Youngman*

Our village idiot bought himself a pet zebra. Named it Spot. —*Henny Youngman*

Of course, our town had a village idiot, too. He could never watch "Jeopardy" unless it came with subtitles.

We had a very unique town idiot. His shoe size and his I.Q. were exactly the same.

This guy was so dumb he could get lost staying home.

One year he went to see Mt. Rushmore and said he wasn't going to go back until they changed the faces.

He also believed it was a natural rock formation.

He didn't drive, but he kept putting nickels in the parking meters. He thought when you put enough money in, they gave you a car.

This guy was so dumb that if his mind suddenly went blank, it was an improvement.

He tattooed his name and address on his forehead so that anytime he got lost he could just mail himself home.

He lost his shoes one day because he put them on the wrong feet. Then he couldn't remember whose feet he put them on.

The proudest day of his life was when he learned how to tie his own shoes. Then he broke his nose. Unfortunately, he'd tied them together.

He says he always has headaches because his hats are too big. Finally someone told him to try using a chin strap instead of a staple gun.

My uncle was the town drunk . . . and we lived in Chicago.
—*George Gobel*

A drunk walked up to a parking meter and put in a dime. The dial went to 60. He said, "How do you like that? I weigh an hour." —*Henny Youngman*

My father was never home; he was always drinking booze. He saw a sign saying, "Drink Canada Dry." So he went up there. —*Henny Youngman*

I only drink to steady my nerves. Last night I got so steady I couldn't move. —*Joe E. Lewis*

My grandfather drank a quart a day and he lived to be 103. I went to his cremation; that fire never did go out.
—*Slappy White*

26

How can I tell when I've had enough to drink? Easy. When my knees start to bend backwards.   —*W. C. Fields*

Our town had a great town drunk. They built a monument to our town drunk. It's a beautiful bronze statue that's lying in the park.

Our town drunk didn't like to shave. He thought it was a terrible waste of shaving lotion.

This guy would drink anything. He's the only guy who ever coated his body with suntan lotion . . . on the inside.

He really would drink anything. He was single-handedly responsible for our town's hair tonic blight of '63.

This guy saw double for all his adult life. He thought the entire town was made up of twins.

He kept wondering where his went.

He was not only the town drunk, he was also the town War Memorial. We couldn't afford an eternal flame so we just set fire to his breath.

And he did his community service. They used to use his breath to kill all the weeds in Town Square.

And in the winter he'd breathe on the interstate highway to melt the snow.

Some good townspeople tried to rehabilitate him and they did pretty well. For awhile there they had him standing on his own two knees.

—— ★ ——

I came from a tough neighborhood. Any cat with a tail was a tourist. —*Milton Berle*

I live in a rough neighborhood. We just put up a sign. It says, "Drive Fast. The life you save may be your own." —*Rodney Dangerfield*

I'll give you an idea how crime-ridden our neighborhood is. The other day I saw half a cop. —*Milton Berle*

Talk about tough neighborhoods. Where I lived nobody asked you the time, they just took your watch. —*Milton Berle*

Where I live, we don't worry about crime in the streets. They make house calls. —*Milton Berle*

★ ★ ★ ★ ★

Our neighborhood was so tough any kid with all his teeth was a sissy.

—— ★ ——

Guys in our neighborhood were so tough they used to steal hubcaps from cars . . . while they were moving.

The first words that babies would speak in our neighborhood were "mama" and "duck."

I went to a very tough school. Every one of my classmates was the school bully.

Anytime I came home from school without a bloody nose my mother knew I played hookey.

I got beat up so much in high school that I went to a four-year college just to heal.

We had so many fights in our school, recess was when we were all sent to a neutral corner.

At our school, the queen of the senior prom was selected by an arm-wrestling competition.

All the pictures in our yearbook were shown front and profile.

Our senior prom didn't need any chaperons. We had enough parole officers to keep order.

Over half the kids in our school graduated on a plea bargain.

On Valentine's Day, we exchanged heart-shaped wanted posters of each other.

"I used to like to go out and paint the town red. Now my brushes are all frayed, and I can't get the lid off the paint can."

—*Gene Perret*

Television is a *medium* . . . so-called because it's neither rare nor well done.
—*Ernie Kovacs*

Who says we didn't have controversial subjects on TV back then? Remember "Bonanza"? It was about three guys in high heels living together.
—*Milton Berle*

I just got my TV set insured. If it breaks down, they send me a pair of binoculars so I can watch my neighbor's set.
—*Henny Youngman*

If it wasn't for electricity, we'd all be watching television by candlelight.
—*George Gobel*

Television is great. You can go on the air and kid the politicians. And the politicians can go on the air and kid the people.
—*Groucho Marx*

I've been watching so many Westerns on television, the legs under my living room chair are permanently bowed.
—*Jack Carter*

Television is like your wife. It's home and it's free.
—*Slappy White*

★　★　★　★　★

Television is nature's way of telling us we should have gone out and done something enjoyable this evening.

Television is something to do without actually doing anything.

—— ★ ——

With cable, some people get a selection of 100 different channels. That means 100 times every half-hour they get to say, "See what else is on."

—— ★ ——

Calling television "entertainment" is like calling falling of a cliff "transportation."

—— ★ ——

Television is radio without the imagination.

—— ★ ——

There are three kinds of television programming: good, bad, and good and bad.

—— ★ ——

Home-shopping shows are very big on television and very convenient. You can now go broke in the comfort of your own living room.

—— ★ ——

Television used to exhibit bad taste. Now, thanks to home shopping, you can have it delivered.

—— ★ ——

Talk shows have been popular on TV for about 15 years now. Pretty soon they're going to say something.

—— ★ ——

Talk shows are informational. They discuss in-depth topics that are of interest to no one.

—— ★ ——

Talk shows can be very educational. For much of my life, I was under the mistaken assumption there were only two sexes.

—— ★ ——

Television will never replace the newspaper. You can't wrap a fish in it.

—— ★ ——

TV talk shows ran out of things to talk about years ago. They just haven't stopped talking yet.

— ★ —

I can't understand why a person would take a year to write a novel when he can easily buy one for a few dollars.
—*Fred Allen*

From the moment I picked your book up until I laid it down, I was convulsed with laughter. Someday I intend to read it.
—*Groucho Marx*

This must be a gift book. That is to say, a book which you wouldn't take on any other terms.
—*Dorothy Parker*

Just got back from the hospital. I was in a speed-reading accident.
—*Steven Wright*

First time I read the dictionary I thought it was a poem about everything.
—*Steven Wright*

I have given up reading books. I find it takes my mind off myself.
—*Oscar Levant*

The covers of this book are too far apart.
—*Ambrose Bierce*

Be careful about reading health books. You may die of a misprint.
—*Mark Twain*

I have one hundred and fifty books, but I have no book-case. Nobody would lend me a bookcase.

—*Henny Youngman*

I went to a bookstore and I asked the clerk where the self-help section was. She said, "If I told you, that would defeat the whole purpose."

—*Brian Kiley*

I love to read a good book before going to sleep, because after going to sleep I keep forgetting to turn the pages.

Books can take you to anyplace in the world, and they have more leg room than most airplanes.

Some say dog is man's best friend; I say books are. You don't have to walk them nor clean up after them.

Two things can ruin a good book for me—having someone tell me the ending or dropping it into the bath water.

I read a book on levitation the other day. I couldn't put it down.

I read a good book on improving your memory. It was called . . . uh . . .

I had a book on improving your memory. I read it twice. I forgot I read it the first time.

I always read the last chapter of mystery novels first. I know who did it, but I have no idea what they did.

I'm a very slow reader. By the time I get to the end of a mystery novel it doesn't matter who did it. The statute of limitations has run out.

I had a friend who once tried to read the local phone book from cover to cover, but he kept losing track of the characters.

I picked up a self-help book that was so complicated I had to get someone to help me read it.

——— ★ ———

I bought a book about near-death experiences, but I took it back. I didn't like the ending.

. . . It didn't seem complete.

——— ★ ———

I've played the harmonica ever since I was big enough to defend myself.　　　　　　　　　　　　　*—Herb Shriner*

Modern music hasn't been around too long and hopefully won't be.　　　　　　　　　　　　　　*—Victor Borge*

Jack Benny is the only fiddler who makes you feel that the strings would sound better back in the cat.　　*—Fred Allen*

I haven't heard singing like that since I was over at the zoo and the moose sat down on the porcupine.
　　　　　　　　　　　　　　　　　　—Amos 'n Andy

The Steinway people have asked me to announce that this is a Baldwin piano.
—*Victor Borge*

My father once tried to play "Flight of the Bumblebee" on the tuba. Blew his liver through the horn. —*Woody Allen*

I see the Beatles have arrived from England. They were forty pounds overweight, and that was just their hair.
—*Bob Hope*

When he plays the piano, I want to get up and dance. Anything is better than just sitting there and listening.

They laughed when I sat down to play. I was facing away from the piano.

He plays the French horn so badly it comes out sounding like Greek.

When he plays the trumpet, the trumpet usually wins.

When he plays classical music, it gives Beethoven a reason to be glad he's deaf.

——— ★ ———

When she sings, she hits notes so high that only dogs can hear them. As far as I'm concerned, that's the dogs' problem.

——— ★ ———

He plays "Flight of the Bumblebee" as if he has already been stung.

——— ★ ———

When I play the guitar, I can clear a room faster than a smoke alarm.

——— ★ ———

He can only play two songs on the piano. One is "Old McDonald Had a Farm" and the other one isn't.

—— ★ ——

When he plays "The Blue Danube," you kind of hope he'll throw himself into it.

—— ★ ——

Some people can play and make you appreciate music. When he plays, he makes you appreciate earplugs.

—— ★ ——

An incurable music lover is someone who will buy a set of drums for their own kid.

—— ★ ——

If my film makes one more person miserable, I'll feel I've done my job.   —*Woody Allen*

The Academy Awards are definitely fixed. The best actress award is always won by a woman.   —*Groucho Marx*

★   ★   ★   ★   ★

It's fun . . . a good movie, a large box of popcorn, a soft drink . . . what better way to spend 30 or 40 dollars?

—— ★ ——

Of course, the large size of popcorn is a very good buy, because once you eat the popcorn, you can have the container made into a summer home.

You used to be able to go into the theater and buy a normal size chocolate bar. Now they sell it by the acre.

Movies make a lot more money today than they used to. Of course, with what you pay for a ticket today, you used to be able to buy a home back then.

It used to be if a film made 7 or 8 million dollars, it was a hit. Now that's what the star's agent gets.

The movie industry made a fortune. The MGM lion doesn't growl anymore. He just smiles and counts.

How about all those horror films? Who ever thought we'd see the day when an actor would write on his résumé: "Can operate a chain saw."

Years ago, the worst violence was a pie in the face. Nowadays you rarely get to keep your face through the entire movie.

Gangster movies are kind of self-defeating. It's hard to prove that crime doesn't pay when you're paying $7.50 a pop to see it.

Years ago movies used to have a story line. Today all they need is a choice of weapons and a list of victims.

All these new action-adventure films have a standard story line—boy meets girl, boy loses girl, boy blows up everybody in the picture.

There are a lot of movies out now aimed at youngsters. They have a special rating. Parents are not admitted unless they have a teenager there to explain it to them.

—— ★ ——

You go to the ballet and you see girls dancing on their toes. Why don't they just get taller girls?   —*Greg Ray*

I was a ballerina. I had to quit after I injured a groin muscle. It wasn't mine.   —*Rita Rudner*

I didn't dig ballet. The last time I went with friends—there was a lot of money bet on the swan to live. —*Woody Allen*

★   ★   ★   ★   ★

Some people say that ballet tells a story. Those are probably the people who stay awake for it.

—— ★ ——

Male dancers wear what they call "ballet tights." If anything that's an understatement.

—— ★ ——

Those costumes are so tight if you have a tattoo, you have to wear it outside your leotards.

—— ★ ——

Ballet demands discipline, skill, athleticism, perseverance, and courage. And that's just to get into the tights.

Ballet dancers always seem to be jumping up in the air. That's because in those tight costumes, it's preferable to bending over.

It's very relaxing to sit in the audience and watch people dance ballet. That's because no matter what you're wearing, it's more comfortable than what they're wearing.

I never danced ballet. The closest I ever came was as a kid walking over hot asphalt in my bare feet.

Some people go to the ballet for the music, some for the dance. And many go because they lost an argument with their spouse.

Ballet dancers are magnificent athletes. Put a ball in their hands and they'd each be worth $4 million a year.

It's not easy to do a *pas-de-deux,* a *tour en l'air,* a *brise,* or a *penche.* A normal person could pull a muscle just trying to spell them.

Probably more American men would enjoy ballet if you could watch it with your shoes off and a six-pack of beer.

. . . And being able to bet on it wouldn't hurt.

I don't understand ballet. I don't understand calculus either, but I've never paid 50 bucks a ticket to go watch calculus.

Opera in English is, in the main, just about as sensible as baseball in Italian.
—*H. L. Mencken*

When an opera star sings her head off, she usually improves her appearance.
—*Victor Borge*

I go to the opera whether I need the sleep or not.
—*Henny Youngman*

★ ★ ★ ★ ★

If I wanted to hear people sing in a foreign language, I would have been born in a foreign country.

—— ★ ——

I go to the opera house because it makes my wife happy. I just wish sometimes she'd come with me.

—— ★ ——

You know who will make a fortune? The person who invents opera with subtitles.

—— ★ ——

The thing I hate most about opera singing is that it usually wakes me up.

—— ★ ——

I would enjoy a good night at the opera if there were such a thing.

I enjoy going to the opera. I enjoy coming home again, too. It's sitting there through the whole thing that gets me.

My spouse takes me to the opera so often I've learned to snore in Italian.

My wife gets upset with me because every time she wants to go to the opera I want to stay home. So I've offered a compromise. I'll go halfway there.

I've finally figured out why operas are all in a foreign language. That's so the guy who wrote them would understand them.

To me, a night at the opera is watching a play I don't like, sung in a language I don't understand, wearing a tuxedo that doesn't fit.

Opera is rap music for highbrows.

I go to the opera regularly. I'm going to keep going until I understand what's happening.

COMING SOON...

HOLIDAYS & SEASONS

"I once wanted to become an atheist, but I gave it up. Not enough holidays."
—*Henny Youngman*

Spring showers in California bring mud slides. That's when you look out the window of your car and find out that your house is making better time than you are.

—*Bob Hope*

★ ★ ★ ★ ★

Spring is when the birds return from their trip south for the winter, and they're all grumpy about having to return from their vacation. —— ★ ——

Birds who migrate are lucky. At least they don't have to make the trip with the kids screaming in the back of the car. —— ★ ——

Some birds don't go south for the winter. I suppose, like the rest of us, they can't afford it.

Spring is when a young man's fancy lightly turns to thoughts of love. For most young men, so is summer, fall, and winter. —— ★ ——

You can almost smell the romance in the air in spring. It's either that or all those "scratch and sniff" ads in the magazines. —— ★ ——

44

Spring is such a gorgeous season because the earth turns green. It blends so beautifully with the brown of our skies.

Spring is a time when the umpire shouts, "Play ball" and the Dodgers shout back, "We're trying, we're trying! . . ."

Spring is when Mother Nature awakens from her long winter's sleep. Thank goodness she's in a better mood when she wakes up than I am.

. . . Otherwise spring would be hell on earth until she's had her second cup of coffee.

If you had to pick a color to symbolize spring it would be green, because it's in spring that taxes are due.

In California, spring is when the swallows return to Capistrano. In the Midwest, it's when feeling returns to your feet.

Spring is a nice time of year. It's when "damn" and "snow" become two separate words again.

Spring, they say, is when a young man's fancy turns to thoughts of love. Of course, I wonder how anyone can think of love with a turned fancy?

I turned my ankle once and couldn't think of anything but getting to a doctor.

Spring is a happy time of life—especially for baseball players. That's when they start collecting their million dollar salaries.

All the birds start returning in spring, which means you probably have to get your car washed more often.

—— ★ ——

All the birds return in spring, which is great unless you happen to be a worm.

. . . especially one who gets up early.

—— ★ ——

Spring is a time of year when the birds and the bees become active again. From what my father told me about them, they should all be in jail.

—— ★ ——

Spring is the time of year when everything turns green— especially the cheese you've had in your refrigerator since last summer.

—— ★ ——

Spring is when everything turns green . . . including my father who knows that income tax time is near.

—— ★ ——

It was so hot the other day, I passed Grant's tomb and the window was open.
                                                        —*Milton Berle*

★   ★   ★   ★   ★

Summer is vacation time. That's when you go away for two weeks and your money goes away forever.

Everyone should take a summer vacation. Remember, mosquitos have to eat, too.

I love summer vacation. It's so relaxing . . . to get back to work again.

I found out what I don't like about family vacations—family.

During the whole drive to our summer vacation, the kids kept asking, "Are we there yet?" Once we arrived they keep asking, "When can we go home?"

My wife wanted to go to Hawaii for our vacation; I wanted to go to Bermuda. So we split the difference. We stayed home.

The heat this summer has been terrible. I took off the clothes I wore yesterday and threw them in the hamper. It threw them back out.

It was so hot today that now I think I have a genuine feel for how Frosty the Snowman feels at the end of the song.

It was so hot in Arizona even the cactuses were checking into hotels for the weekend.

——— ★ ———

It's been so hot lately they had to put sandbags around the Hollywood Wax Museum. If Roseanne Arnold melts she could wipe out Sunset Boulevard.

——— ★ ———

It was so hot in Palm Springs even the lizards were wearing Bermuda shorts.

It's been hot lately. I've got underarm stains on clothes I haven't even taken out of the closet yet.

Fall is my favorite season in Los Angeles, watching the birds change color and fall from the trees.

—*David Letterman*

It's nice to work in New York City in the fall. It's nice to walk down Madison Avenue and see the trees turning from charcoal gray to charcoal brown.　　—*Joe E. Lewis*

★　★　★　★　★

Every year in fall many things in nature turn to pretty orange, yellow, red, and brown. I have things in my refrigerator that do that every month.

Fall is a time of glorious color. It's the season when Mother Nature thinks she's Ted Turner.

If Mother Nature wanted autumn to be really beautiful, she would have raked up the leaves herself.

—— ★ ——

My wife loves it when the leaves turn all different colors. Yet she got very upset when the ring I bought her did the same thing.

In fall the leaves turn different colors and get immortalized by poets. When your teeth do that, you get a lecture from your dentist.

Autumn is when the leaves turn and fall. I have an uncle who does that every time he tries to leave the corner bar.

Every autumn I watch the first leaf fall from the tree. I watch it float gracefully downward and land softly on the earth. I turn and hear my wife say, "Don't you think it's about time you raked the lawn?"

Fall is when the leaves on the trees know their usefulness is done and they depart gracefully. Politicians should be made to watch and learn.

In fall the trees go from having plenty of leaves to having none at all. For us humans, that happens at tax time.

The autumn leaves turn deep brown and get dry and brittle. It reminds me a lot of my cooking.

In autumn all of nature turns glorious, brilliant, vibrant colors. You can get the same effect stubbing your toe in a dark bedroom.

In fall all of nature keeps turning different and unusual colors. It reminds me of a cheap watchband I once bought.

. . . It didn't last through the winter, either.

My wife is always after me to rake up the leaves. I'm always saying, "Wait a few months; the snow will cover them."

—— ★ ——

I hate raking leaves. It would be a lot easier if the birds would stay here, and the trees on my lawn would go south for the winter.

—— ★ ——

Fall is a time when nature turns many different shades and then loses everything. You and I do the same thing when we get seasick.

—— ★ ——

The trees lose all of their leaves in the fall. It's strange. They're the only things that get undressed for winter.

—— ★ ——

In autumn the leaves turn different colors and begin to fall. I have an Uncle George who does that every Friday evening.

—— ★ ——

I think nature is very inconsiderate in fall. I can understand the trees losing their foliage. I went bald several years ago, but I didn't leave my hair lying all over someone's lawn.

—— ★ ——

I don't want to find fault, but I wonder if God ever considered having snow fall up?

—*Robert Orben*

50

A lot of people like snow. I find it an unnecessary freezing of water.   —*Carl Reiner*

It's so cold here a pin-up calendar isn't a luxury, it's a necessity.   —*Bob Hope*

It was so cold that even politicians were walking around with their hands in their own pockets.   —*Bob Hope*

This town only had two seasons—winter and "Road Under Repair."   —*George Gobel*

It was so cold that our words came out as ice cubes. We had to throw them on the fire and melt them to hear what we were saying.   —*Joe Perret*

It's been a very harsh winter. On Groundhog Day, the groundhog not only wouldn't look for his shadow, he re-fused to leave his electric blanket.

The harsh winter storms paralyzed some of our towns. No telephones, no power. They only way you could get a mes-sage across town was to hire a homing penguin.

What a cold winter. In the Midwest they've been shoveling so much it feels like a presidential election year.

It was a cold winter this year. The only explanation is that Jack Frost must be on steroids.

It was so cold this winter that in parts of the Midwest, Sterno has become an after-dinner drink.

This has been a very bitter winter. In parts of the North, a favorite pastime was sitting in your living room trying to remember what your toes felt like.

Of course, it's always warm in Southern California. There when people shiver it means they're having an earthquake.

Of course, the bitter winter keeps the parks a little cleaner. It's too cold for a pigeon to sit on a statue in that weather.

It's been very cold this winter. I saw the first robin of spring and he was wearing an overcoat.

The tough winter causes a lot of illnesses, too. This year the flu bug stayed around longer than most new television shows.

We only had one minor problem on July 4th. We had to ask the kids to turn down their stereo so we could hear the fireworks.
—*Robert Orben*

Every Fourth of July, we'd give my uncle a hotfoot while he was sleeping. His language when he woke up was the only fireworks we could afford.

The Fourth of July is a tribute to America. Thanks to American politicians, we cannot only put over 200 candles on our cake, but we also have enough hot air to blow them out.

It's a funny thing about our nation: July 4th is its birthday, but April 15th is when it collects the presents.

Can you imagine if our Founding Fathers could see this country today. They'd look at the smog and think the English were trying to win the Revolution with germ warfare.

. . . They'd look at all the nudity in our movies and wonder why Betsy Ross gave up sewing.

. . . They'd see all our traffic jams and be glad that Paul Revere rode a horse.

. . . They'd see the costumes that some of our teenage girls wear and know why our national anthem begins "Oh say, can you see . . ."

There are two sounds you hear an awful lot of on July 4th: firecrackers going off and ants licking their chops.

Everybody eats outdoors on this holiday. It's an unwritten law: the Fourth of July is the oven's day off.

The Fourth of July comes in the middle of the summer, but it's not the longest day of the year. It only seems that way when you're trying to light the charcoal.

We have some of the worst chefs in the world cooking outdoors on July 4th. If you don't believe me, just watch the flies in the evening. They buzz around the medicine chest.

My Dad always used to cook outdoors on the Fourth of July. *Medium rare* meant you got your steak before the fire department came.

You can always tell a good barbecue chef. He's the one who still has eyebrows when he's done.

The biggest cause of injury at the Fourth of July picnic is food inhalation.

If you really want to eat a good meal outdoors on the Fourth of July, be a mosquito.

I went to a Halloween party dressed as the equator. As people walked towards me they got warmer.
—*Steven Wright*

I was so ugly as a kid, I had to trick-or-treat over the phone.
—*Rodney Dangerfield*

I was so ugly as a kid we never had a jack-o'-lantern. They just stuck me in the window.　　　—*Rodney Dangerfield*

I always used to scare the neighbors on Halloween. I dressed up as my brother.

Halloween is an educational holiday. If it weren't for that day none of us would know what a goblin looked like.

I love Halloween. The Christmas decorations look so nice in the department stores.

Halloween is when people try to frighten you into giving them goodies. In some ways, it's a lot like government.

I know one girl who was so skinny, on Halloween she'd wear nothing but a white, fuzzy hat and a white, fuzzy slippers and go trick-or-treating as a Q-Tip.

I know one guy who was tall, slender, and bald. On Halloween he'd paint his head blue and go to the party as a ballpoint pen.

Women who are looking for Mr. Right enjoy Halloween. For that one night, at least, they can settle for Mr. "You-don't-look-half-bad-with-a-mask-on."

Halloween is not a big holiday at most nudist camps. It's hard to dress up where no clothes are allowed.

. . . Besides, even with a mask, people can usually tell who you are.

Halloween is when you're constantly threatened with "trick or treat." It has a lot in common with election night, doesn't it?

—— ★ ——

Halloween is a night when everyone tries to look grotesque, as opposed to the rest of the year when only rock stars do.

—— ★ ——

Santa Claus has the right idea. Visit people once a year.
—*Victor Borge*

This guy is so cheap he sends one Christmas card out each year . . . in the form of a chain letter. —*Phyllis Diller*

I gave my wife a brand new watch for Christmas—waterproof, shockproof, unbreakable, and anti-magnetic. Absolutely nothing could happen to it—she lost it.
—*Milton Berle*

As my children got older, I got used to buying Christmas presents that (A) I couldn't spell, (B) Had no idea what they were used for, and (C) Leaked grease.
—*Erma Bombeck*

★　★　★　★　★

For Christmas, my wife gave me a gift that had thousands of dollars written all over it. It was a handful of wanted posters.

—— ★ ——

I know some parents who were very smart. They bought their kids some batteries for Christmas and put a sign on them that said, "Toys not included."

—— ★ ——

The crowds in department stores are horrifying this time of year. I had a pleasant time shopping the other day . . . That means I finished in the same clothes I started in.

—— ★ ——

Christmas is the time to eat, drink, and be merry, because starting tomorrow, you'll be doing nothing else except watching bowl games.

—— ★ ——

Of course, football is a contact sport . . . just like Christmas shopping.

—— ★ ——

Christmas is that time of year when everybody is happy, cheerful, bright, and merry. It's like any weekend at a fraternity house.

—— ★ ——

Christmas season is starting to last longer than the basketball season.

—— ★ ——

The stores love it when the bells we hear at Christmas are from a cash register.

—— ★ ——

Early Christmas is great for kids. They can sit on Santa's knee, tell him they've been a good little boy, then go home and have three months of hell-raising before the presents arrive.

—— ★ ——

The stores are saying this year, "It's better to give than to receive. . . . So give me your cash, your checks, or your credit cards."

—— ★ ——

We got the kids something nice for Christmas—their own apartment.

— ★ —

New Year's Eve . . . "where auld acquaintance be forgot"— unless those tests come back positive.　　　　—*Jay Leno*

★　　★　　★　　★　　★

New Year's Eve is a night when we all sing "Auld Lang Syne" from the heart . . . which is not easy since none of us knows what it means.

— ★ —

New Year's Eve is that night when we should all take one serious moment to tell each other how silly we all look in those party hats.

— ★ —

The morning after the New Year's Eve party is when you wake up to find the old year erased from your memory . . . along with your name and where you left your car.

— ★ —

You know you're getting too old for wild New Year's Eve parties when you meet the Old Year on his way out and he looks younger than you do.

— ★ —

The nice thing about wild New Year's Eve parties is that when you wake up the next morning you know that from that point on the year has got to get better.

———— ★ ————

New Year's Eve is a functional holiday. After Thanksgiving and Christmas, this is the night that you finally wash down the turkey.

———— ★ ————

New Year's resolutions are like the glass in fire alarms—they're only made to be broken.

———— ★ ————

Making New Year's resolutions is like holding onto a hot coal. It takes courage to try it, but it feels so damn good when you drop it.

———— ★ ————

I made a New Year's resolution to be kind, considerate, and nice. Then I decided, nah, I'd rather be myself.

———— ★ ————

New Year's resolutions are the only things in the world that are broken faster than the rules in a wrestling match.

———— ★ ————

I killed two birds with one stone this year: I gave up New Year's resolutions for Lent.

———— ★ ————

I know one guy who watched so much football on television on New Year's Day that his wife finally came in and gave him the two minute warning on their marriage.

———— ★ ————

I know one friend who glues himself to the television set to watch football all New Year's Day. Last January it took him three days to get the astroturf stains off the tip of his nose.

———— ★ ————

It's always sad to ring out the old year. It means you can't get any more deductions on your tax returns.

———— ★ ————

SOON TO APPEAR—

MONEY

"Money is better than poverty,
if only for financial reasons."
—*Woody Allen*

Politics has become so expensive that it takes a lot of money even to be defeated.
—*Will Rogers*

At today's prices you're lucky if you can make one end meet.
—*Milton Berle*

Among the things that money can't buy is what it used to.
—*Max Kaufman*

My wife and I were considering a divorce, but after pricing lawyers we decided to buy a new car instead.
—*Henny Youngman*

I'm paying so much insurance to take care of the future that I'm starving to death in the present.
—*Alan King*

Flying is so expensive these days. I took an economy flight. There wasn't any movie, but they flew low over the drive-ins.
—*Red Buttons*

★　★　★　★　★

Funerals are so expensive. When my uncle died, my aunt couldn't afford a casket; so, she bought him a suit with six handles.

Extreme wealth used to be a status symbol. Now it's a necessity just to make ends meet.

A Rolex watch costs between 4 and 20 thousand dollars. I don't want to know the time that bad.

. . . It's cheaper to carry a pocket full of quarters and just dial 555-TIME.

—— ★ ——

Everyone should have a roof over their head. If you also want walls and a floor you may be getting out of your price range.

—— ★ ——

Women are worried about who's going to care for their kids while they work. That shouldn't be a problem much longer. With today's housing costs, even the kids will have to find jobs.

—— ★ ——

You go into a realtor today and say, "What can you show me for $50,000?" They show you the door.

—— ★ ——

Millionaire used to mean a rich man. Today it just means a guy who might own his own home.

—— ★ ——

Sporting events are getting expensive. Soon the fans will have to decide whether to go to the game, or send their kids to college.

—— ★ ——

Inflation is when the buck doesn't stop anywhere.
—*Robert Orben*

Inflation has hit everything. Pillow down is up, Macy's basement is now on the fourth floor, and pumpernickel is now pumperdime.
—*Marty Brill*

Inflation is when you're wealthy and you no longer can afford the things you bought when you were poor.
—*Robert Orben*

Inflation—that's when prices go from reasonable to expensive to "How much have you got with you?"
—*Bob Hope*

I joined an organization that fights inflation. An hour after I joined, they raised the dues.
—*Milton Berle*

I don't mind going back to daylight savings time. With inflation, the hour will be the only thing I've saved this year.
—*Victor Borge*

Inflation: When Congress becomes ten percent efficient, why, that is inflation.
—*Will Rogers*

Americans are getting stronger. Twenty years ago it took two people to carry ten dollars worth of groceries. Today a five-year-old can do it.
—*Henny Youngman*

Times are so bad nowadays, even people who don't intend to pay ain't buying.
—*Slappy White*

I figure inflation is really here. I gave my nephew a nickel and he asked, "What is this thing—a medal?"
—*Pat Cooper*

★　★　★　★　★

Inflation has driven the value of our money down so much that now even muggers won't accept cash.

Inflation means if you put off 'til tomorrow what you could do today, you might not be able to afford to do it.

Inflation is when things cost more and are worth less. That also describes most souvenir shops.

Inflation is when everything you have is worth more, except you.

One way to beat inflation is if you need something today, buy it tomorrow at yesterday's prices.

Costs have gone up so much they've changed the Lord's Prayer to "Give us this day our daily bread plus shipping and handling."

Prices have gone up so much that nowadays only the rich can afford to act like the middle class.

One good thing about inflation: poverty is now affordable to everyone.

Everything costs so much today that they've now come up with a wallet that fits conveniently under the seat in front of you or in the overhead compartment.

Things cost so much nowadays that some people want to get shoplifting reduced from a misdemeanor to a necessity.

Inflation is terrible. Interest is worth more than money nowadays.

Inflation continues to go up. They used to say that money can't buy happiness. Today it can't even buy groceries.

Prices are getting ridiculous. Supermarkets now have a bag boy to help you carry the money *in*.

Inflation means your money can't buy as much today as it did yesterday. My money can't buy anything today; I spent it all yesterday.

Inflation means when you save up for your old age, you go broke when you're middle-aged.

Inflation is getting so bad that nowadays not even the Joneses can afford to keep up with the Joneses.

Inflation means you can still buy a good 5-cent cigar, but it costs you $1.75.

Look on the bright side of inflation. If you could have lived in the 18th century, you would have been rich by now.

Inflation is kind of hard to explain. Think of it as termites of the wallet.

Inflation means if you're worth nothing today, you'll be worth less tomorrow.

Inflation means that this year's money will someday be worth as much as last year's calendar.

My dad said when he was a kid, milk was only 2 cents a quart. I don't know why he didn't buy a whole lot of it then, and save it.

SAVING MONEY

I don't have a savings account because . . . I don't know my mother's maiden name.   —*Paula Poundstone*

I try to save my money. Who knows? Maybe one day it'll become valuable again.   —*Milton Berle*

My wife will buy anything marked down. Yesterday, she tried to buy an escalator.   —*Joey Bishop*

And when it comes to sales, my wife is the all-time champion. Our local supermarket now advertises sales by posters that say, "Dear Mrs. King . . ."   —*Alan King*

My wife makes the budget work. We do without a lot of things I don't need.   —*Milton Berle*

Save a little money each month, and at the end of the year, you'll be surprised at how little you have.
          —*Ernest Haskins*

My father originated the limbo dance—trying to get into a pay toilet.   —*Slappy White*

My wife loves bargains. What a great shopper! One time she went out window shopping—came home with seven windows.   —*Alan King*

If there was ever a time to save money, it's now. When a dog gets a bone, he don't go out and make the first payment on a bigger bone. He buries the one he's got.

—*Will Rogers*

I tried to save grocery money once, but some of the suggestions were just not practical, like "Don't shop when you're hungry," which eliminated all hours when the store was open.

—*Erma Bombeck*

I've been trying to save up for a rainy day. So far I can handle a light mist.

I've been saving for a rainy day. I'm happy to say in two more years I can buy that umbrella.

I always throw my loose change into a large vase because my mother always told me "a penny saved is a penny urned."

Two can live as cheaply as one . . . if one of them doesn't eat.

I finally saved up enough money to do something I've been meaning to do since 1960. I bought a 1960 Cadillac.

I finally saved up enough to open a savings account at the bank. The toaster they gave me set fire to my kitchen.

I withdrew my life savings from the bank. The teller asked, "How would you like that? Heads or tails?"

I've saved for years and years. Do you know what I got? Older.

—— ★ ——

My grandparents lost their life savings by taking a cruise. What grandpop thought was a wall safe turned out to be a porthole.

—— ★ ——

I try to save by clipping coupons. Last week alone, I got about 50 or 60 paper cuts.

—— ★ ——

My bank not only pays next to nothing on my savings account, but the calendar they sent me for Christmas only has 13 days in each month.

—— ★ ——

I always carry a little cash that I call "mad money." Every time I look at it, it makes me mad that I don't have more.

—— ★ ——

When Coolidge was president, men bought stocks who had never even bought toothpaste before. —*Will Rogers*

The past few weeks Wall Street has gone into one tailspin after another. You would pick up the morning paper, read the stock report and wouldn't think there was that many minus signs in the world. —*Will Rogers*

My father was a very successful businessman but he was ruined in the stock market crash. . . . A big stockbroker jumped out the window and fell on his pushcart.
—*Jackie Mason*

There are two times in a man's life when he should not speculate: when he can afford it and when he can't.
—*Mark Twain*

A stockbroker is a man who runs your fortune into a shoe-string.
—*Alexander Woollcott*

I called my broker yesterday and he put me on hold. By the time he got back on the phone, I had nothing left to talk to him about.

I lost so much money in the market this year, I can afford to tell the truth on my tax return.

Wall Street is in a "slump." It doesn't become a "catastrophe" until it's their own money they start losing.

Wall Street is expecting the worst. The last time I saw my broker he was wearing a crash helmet.

The stock market performed so badly today, I went down to Wall Street and laid a wreath on my money.

Wall Street must be doing badly today. I tried to call my broker and he wouldn't accept the charges.

I tried to check how my stocks were doing in the newspaper. I had to keep switching back and forth from the "financial page" to the "obituaries."

The only things I read in the newspaper anymore are the comic pages and the stock market—the funnies and the saddies.

———— ★ ————

I called my stockbroker and asked how badly my investments were doing. He said, "In five seconds, your credit cards will self-destruct."

———— ★ ————

I lost so much money so fast in the stock market today, my wallet has skid marks on it.

———— ★ ————

It's not real hard to find my stocks on the financial page. They're the ones that are trimmed in black.

———— ★ ————

My stocks are doing very badly right about now. I used to shower every day; now I take a bath, too.

———— ★ ————

When I first heard how badly the stock market was doing, I tried to call my broker, but his ledge was busy.

———— ★ ————

The stock market went down fast, and a lot of people in Beverly Hills lost quite a bit of money. People there now have their chauffeurs drop them off at a soup kitchen.

———— ★ ————

The stock market fell so badly it even hurt Hollywood. Tinseltown can't even afford real tinsel.

———— ★ ————

Johnny Carson was hurt real badly by the stock market decline. It's the most money he's lost and still been married to the same woman.

———— ★ ————

So many people want to get rich quick. I'm not like that. I want to get rich *now*.

———— ★ ————

UP NEXT

AROUND THE HOUSE

"Home, nowadays, is a place where part of the family waits till the rest of the family brings the car back."
—*Earl Wilson*

HOUSEWIVES

I don't like to called "housewife." . . . I prefer "domestic goddess."
—*Roseanne Barr*

My wife does wonderful things with leftovers—she throws them out.
—*Herb Shriner*

Housework can kill you if done right.   —*Erma Bombeck*

★   ★   ★   ★   ★

You can always tell the housewives from the sweethearts in restaurants. The woman buttering six pieces of bread and passing them clockwise around the table . . . housewife.

—— ★ ——

Mom put so much starch in everything. I remember one time I sneezed and cut my nose on the handkerchief.

. . . One night my brother fell out of bed and broke his pajamas.

—— ★ ——

Try this. Leave the dishes undone, the clothes unwashed, throw trash and garbage all over the house. Then when your husband asks what you've been doing all day, say, "Here it is; I didn't do it?"

—— ★ ——

The only question a man asks after "Will you marry me?" is "What's for dinner?"

—— ★ ——

It all evens out. Some women subtract five years from their age, but being a housewife adds ten.

Whoever thinks a housewife has no superiors to answer to has never raised children.

Housewife is a profession, just like being a doctor or a lawyer. Although, if you have several children it's more like being an Indian chief.

Housewife is a very important profession. If it weren't for them we'd all be up to our armpits in dirty laundry.

. . . eating off paper plates.

. . . and never knowing which shirt goes with which pair of trousers.

My wife is an interior decorator. She wants to get rid of me because I clash with the drapes. —*Morey Amsterdam*

When I was a kid, we were evicted so often we had to buy curtains that matched the sidewalks. —*Milton Berle*

Our living room has striped furniture with polka dot wallpaper. It doesn't look pretty, but our company never stays too long.

We had our whole house done in stripes. Good fashion sense prevented the kids from getting the measles.

We had our bedroom and bathroom done entirely in plush, white carpeting. If I nick myself shaving, I have to go to the neighbors' house to bleed.

Everything in our house is neutral except my mother-in-law.

We did our family room entirely in plaids. First thing that happened was my son's pet chameleon had a nervous breakdown.

We wanted a house that looked "lived in," so we bought all our furniture from the YMCA.

We decorated our den entirely in black. First thing I lost was my bowling ball.

We decorated our house in such authentic earth tones that now every August the leaves fall off our dining room table.

I told the decorator I wanted the home to "be me." She added a bay window.

I told the decorator I wanted an office that reflected my work habits. He took out the desk and put in a daybed.

When Sears comes out with a riding vacuum cleaner, then I'll clean the house. —*Roseanne Barr*

My wife forgot this year that she has a microwave oven. You ever eat Thanksgiving dinner at seven in the morning? —*Robert Orben*

My wife gets mixed up with all the gadgets in the kitchen. Yesterday she tried to defrost the stove. —*Milton Berle*

This guy just invented a new microwave television set. He can watch "60 Minutes" in twelve seconds. —*Milton Berle*

Appliance Salesman: You'll like this range. For instance, you put in a roast, you set the oven control, then you go out all day. When you come home at night, the roast is done.

Gracie Allen: Haven't you got one where I don't have to go out? —*Gracie Allen*

★　★　★　★　★

Modern appliances are great. Our new toaster has four different dials on it, which means it has 9,999 different ways to burn toast.

—— ★ ——

Our new juicer makes juice from anything. This morning I had a glass of toast.

—— ★ ——

We have a self-cleaning oven in our kitchen. Big deal. We've had a cat like that for years.

You can't put plastic in the dishwasher, metal in the microwave, utensils in the garbage disposal. There are so many rules in the kitchen, we find it safer to eat out.

I make a peanut-butter sandwich in the microwave oven. It sticks to the roof of your mouth faster.

I don't like cooking in the microwave. It just means you have to do the dishes that much sooner.

The microwave oven is probably the greatest time-saving device since telling my husband to stay out of the kitchen.

Three of the greatest kitchen time-savers are the self-cleaning oven, the self-defrosting refrigerator, and the self-cooking husband.

We have so many appliances in the kitchen that I feel out of place there unless I'm plugged in.

Years ago, I remember my father coming home from work and saying to my mother, "I'm sick and tired of you bending over a hot stove in the kitchen all day. Straighten up."

Everything in our kitchen is automatic and has a timer. My wife could leave me tomorrow and I'd still eat well through next Tuesday.

PRESENTING

WORDS OF WISDOM

"A man begins cutting his wisdom teeth the first time he bites off more than he can chew."

—*Herb Caen*

PHILOSOPHY

To err is human, but it feels divine.　　　*—Mae West*

If you're going to do something tonight that you'll be sorry for tomorrow—sleep late.　　　*—Henny Youngman*

Be good and you will be lonely.　　　*—Mark Twain*

Some people go to India to find the mystery of life. I'm still trying to figure out how to start my car.
　　　—Rodney Dangerfield

An uneasy conscience is a hair in the mouth.
　　　—Mark Twain

Honesty is the best policy, but it is not the cheapest.
　　　—Mark Twain

My grandfather always told me "Don't guard your money; guard your health." While I was busy guarding my health, my grandfather stole my money.　　　*—Jackie Mason*

Let us endeavor so to live that when we come to die even the undertaker will be sorry.　　　*—Mark Twain*

★　　★　　★　　★　　★

Cast your bread upon the water and it will come back to you a hundredfold. What you're going to do with 100 loaves of wet bread is your problem.

All work and no play makes Jack a dull boy—but a helluva lot richer than you are.

My grandfather used to say I couldn't see the forest for the trees. I didn't pay much attention to him, though. He couldn't see the forest for his hangover.

"The early bird," they say, "catches the worm." I say let him have it. I'll sleep in and settle for sausage and eggs.

I never understood that admonition: "The early bird catches the worm." It doesn't say much for the early worm, does it?

Here are a few other little known, but wise admonitions:

. . . If you're going to jump across a well, try to do it in one jump or less.

. . . Never eat in a restaurant where antacid is listed on the menu as a side dish.

. . . Never entrust your life to a surgeon with more than three Band-Aids on his fingers.

. . . Never go to a plastic surgeon whose favorite artist is Picasso.

. . . Never get in line at the bank behind a person wearing a ski mask.

. . . If a band of motorcyclists all wearing black leather vests and covered with tattoos cuts you off on the highway, just think the obscenities quietly to yourself.

. . . If you have nothing good to say about someone, go on an afternoon talk show and say it anyway.

I have a telescope on the peephole of my door; so, I can see who's at the door for 200 miles.　—*Steven Wright*

★　★　★　★　★

Cautious is never making the same mistake once.

I know a man who is overly cautious. He won't even walk the straight and narrow without a safety net under him.

My grandfather always said the best advice he ever heard was "Look before you leap." He thought it explained why there were so few blind pole vaulters.

My grandmother was always careful never to date a man who chewed tobacco. "If he got fresh with you," she said, "you had to think twice before slapping his face."

A friend of mine is a very cautious driver. He drives so slowly, he can change a flat tire without losing time.

I have a friend who's very cautious. He's so afraid of flying he refuses to ride the train. He's afraid an airplane will fall on it.

I know one guy who was so cautious he would only go out after dark because he was afraid of his own shadow.

—— ★ ——

This guy was afraid of his own shadow. Of course, he had reason to be—it looked exactly like him.

—— ★ ——

I know one guy who was so afraid of his own shadow he made it walk 10 paces behind him.

—— ★ ——

Another guy was so afraid of his own shadow, he used to stop and look in a window until it passed.

—— ★ ——

You show me a man who's afraid to take a chance, and I'll show you a man who will probably never win the lottery.

—— ★ ——

People who live in glass houses might as well answer the door.   —*Morey Amsterdam*

Parking is such street sorrow.   —*Herb Caen*

A man in the house is worth two in the street.
                                 —*Mae West*

If at first you don't succeed, I'd stay away from skydiving.
                                 —*Milton Berle*

What is worth doing is worth the trouble of asking somebody to do it.   —*Ambrose Bierce*

You can lead a horse to water, but just stop to think how a wet horse smells. —*George Gobel*

If at first you don't succeed, appoint a committee and let them worry about it. —— ★ ——

A stitch in time can sometimes save embarrassment.

Keep your eye on the ball, your nose to the grindstone, your shoulder to the wheel, and if you can work in that position, you're a better person than I am.

If you can't see the forest for the trees, try looking around for a forest that doesn't have any trees.

Monkey see, monkey do. I don't know what that means. I'm only putting it in here because I've seen it in other books. —— ★ ——

Neither a borrower nor a lender be. That kind of kills any fun you were going to have with the stock market, doesn't it? —— ★ ——

Do unto others before they get a chance to do unto you.

A penny saved is a penny earned. You don't have to take my word on that . . . call the IRS.

A rolling stone gathers no moss. How you react to that statement depends on whether or not you have a worthwhile use for moss. —— ★ ——

You can lead a horse to water, but if you really want to make him drink, put out a bowl of beer nuts first.

—— ★ ——

If at first you don't succeed, start looking around for someone to blame.

—— ★ ——

I still say if God had meant us to eat peanut butter, he would have given us Teflon gums. —*Robert Orben*

I came across a tribe of cannibals who'd been converted by Roman Catholic missionaries. Now, on Friday, they only eat fishermen. —*Max Kaufman*

I'm going to memorize your name and throw my head away. —*Oscar Levant*

I bought a tube of Krazy Glue and the label fell off.
—*Jay Leno*

I just heard from Bill Bailey. He's not coming home.
—*Henny Youngman*

The latest invention I've heard about is a toothpaste with built-in food particles for people who can't eat between every brushing. —*Henny Youngman*

I like to skate on the other side of the ice —*Steven Wright*

Luther Burbank crossed a potato with a sponge. He got something that tastes awful, but it holds a lot of gravy.

—*Doodles Weaver*

I invented a square bathtub which cannot leave a ring.

—*Jackie Vernon*

I had this great idea to make the Great Wall of China into a handball court.

—*George Gobel*

Two kangaroos are talking to each other, and one says, "Gee, I hope it doesn't rain today, I just hate it when the children play inside."

—*Henny Youngman*

Today you can go to a gas station and find the cash register open and the toilets locked.

—*Joey Bishop*

I'm an expert on Chinese food. When I eat it I only use one chopstick.

—*George Burns*

I always buy suits that are too small for me. Then when they don't fit, I don't feel obliged to go on a diet.

I wore a turtle-neck sweater once. When I lay on my back, I found out I couldn't roll over.

I went to a paint store once and they had handicapped parking spaces for people who were color blind.

I go to a very inexpensive doctor. He's an externist.

I know a guy who says he's going to be an atheist all his life . . . God willing.

This world is so unfair. Otherwise, why do the rich people have all the money?

—— ★ ——

My friend's fear of flying eventually killed him. At the airport, an insurance vending machine fell on him.

—— ★ ——

A friend of mine became a podiatrist. When he was going to medical school he didn't want to buy the whole skeleton.

—— ★ ——

My uncle crossed pancake batter with popcorn. He invented flapjacks that flip themselves.

—— ★ ——

My mother always wanted a dishwasher but we couldn't afford it. Dad bought her a bunch of paper plates and an eraser.

—— ★ ——

SILLY THINGS TO PONDER

What's right is what's left if you do everything else wrong.
—*Robin Williams*

What do you send a sick florist? —*Henny Youngman*

Has any turtle ever outlived the shaker of turtle food?
—*Jerry Seinfeld*

Do you ever wonder if illiterate people get the full effect of alphabet soup? —*John Mendoza*

If you shoot at mimes, should you use a silencer?
—*Steven Wright*

How come it's a penny for your thoughts, but you have to put in your 2-cents' worth? Somebody's making a penny.
—*Steven Wright*

How come when you mix flour and water together you get glue? And when you add eggs and sugar, you get a cake? Where does the glue go?   —*Rita Rudner*

Did you ever notice when you blow in a dog's face he gets mad at you, but when you take him in a car he sticks his head out the window?   —*Steve Bluestein*

I'm desperately trying to figure out why kamikaze pilots wore helmets.   —*Dave Edison*

★   ★   ★   ★   ★

What's another word for *thesaurus*?

What time is check-out time in a roach motel?

Why don't fish have to wait an hour after they eat to go swimming again?

What I want to know is when Noah had the two flies on the ark, why didn't he swat them?

And when there were only two aardvarks on Noah's ark, why didn't they have their name legally changed then?

. . . to something easier to spell.

The aardvark has a long snout and a very long tongue. I wonder if it needs both of these just so it's able to pronounce its own name?

If the law of gravity is ever repealed, which may would we all fall?

If a boomerang always comes back to you when you throw it, why throw it in the first place?

A boomerang is a stick that will always come back to you when you throw it. Maybe it's for kids who like to play "fetch," but don't own a dog.

What happens if you want to become a tree surgeon then discover that you can't stand the sight of sap?

If love makes the world go round, why can't I save a few bucks and get it to run my car?

If the number 8 decided to grow long hair and wear an earring, would it then become an odd number?

When you get right down to it, don't you always find anything in the "last place you look for it?"

. . . Once you've found it, why look in another place?

If you put a coffee table in your bedroom, would it keep you up at night?

We all know what it feels like when your foot falls asleep. But does anyone know what it feels like to be asleep and have your foot wake up?

If God gets amnesia, does that make Him an atheist?

"If opposites attracted, the North Pole and the South Pole would be married and living happily at the equator."

—*Gene Perret*

SHORT & TALL

I started show business when I was fourteen and only the size of a kid of ten. By twenty, though, I'd shot up to the size of a kid of eleven. —*Morey Amsterdam*

I feel sorry for short people, you know. When it rains, they're the last to know. —*Rodney Dangerfield*

He's the only man I know that can milk a cow standing up. —*Fred Allen*

I'm not fat at all. . . . I'm just short for my weight. I should be 9'7". —*Totie Fields*

★　★　★　★　★

He was so tiny, he could wear a short-sleeve shirt with French cuffs.

—— ★ ——

He was so short he had to stand on a chair to change his mind.

—— ★ ——

He was so short he could get lost in shag carpeting.

—— ★ ——

I won't say he was short, but he could look for his shoes under the bed without bending over.

—— ★ ——

He was so short he had to grow another 6 inches before his friends would call him "Shorty."

—— ★ ——

89

It was annoying how he was always complaining about being so short. So one day I just stepped on him.

— ★ —

He was so tall that when he fell down, he had to make two trips.

— ★ —

He was so tall when he bent over to tie his shoelaces, his feet would have to meet him halfway.

— ★ —

He was so tall he had a schooner tattooed on his chest . . . actual size.

— ★ —

He was very tall and thin. He looked like a flagpole with hair.

— ★ —

I often quote myself. It adds spice to my conversation.
—*George Bernard Shaw*

I can live for two months on a good compliment.
—*Mark Twain*

Every time I leave the house, my wife tells me to call her in case something goes right. —*Rodney Dangerfield*

He has a terrible inferiority complex and he's right.
—*Milton Berle*

I get no respect. I get mail that starts, "You may already be a loser."
—Rodney Dangerfield

My mother always taught me to be kind to my inferiors, but she never told me what to do when I was in a room where I didn't have any.
—Bob Hope

Dial-a-Prayer hung up on me.
—Jackie Vernon

The meek shall inherit the earth. They won't have the nerve to refuse it.
—Jackie Vernon

Do you ever feel like the whole world's a tuxedo and you're a pair of brown shoes?
—George Gobel

I have no self-confidence. When girls tell me yes, I tell them to think it over.
—Rodney Dangerfield

My only regret in life is that I'm not someone else.
—Woody Allen

★　　★　　★　　★　　★

I know a guy who has such an ego that when he prays he says, "Dear God, do you need anything?"

This guy thinks he's just a little better than everybody else. When he spells his name, he capitalizes the first *two* letters.

This gentleman has such a big head that when he wears a ten-gallon hat, it's one gallon too small.

His head is so big his ears are in separate zip codes.

This guy admits he has no humility, but if he did have it, it would be better than everybody else's.

No matter what this guy does, he thinks that no one can hold a candle to him, although a lot of people would like to.

—— ★ ——

Here's a guy with a giant ego. When he went to see Mt. Rushmore his first words were, "Hey guys, move over."

—— ★ ——

This guy's ego is so big that when he gets on a plane, it won't fit in the overhead compartment.

—— ★ ——

This guy casts two shadows—one for him and one for his ego.

—— ★ ——

His ego is so big that it comes with its own carrying case.

. . . If it weren't on wheels, he couldn't get it around.

—— ★ ——

This guy once wrote a book called *The Ten Greatest People in History and My Views on the Other Nine.*

—— ★ ——

I'd like to have an inferiority complex, but I don't think I'm good enough.

—— ★ ——

I thought I had an inferiority complex, but it turned out to be just good judgment.

—— ★ ——

I know a lot of people with inferiority complexes, but theirs are all better than mine.

—— ★ ——

There's only one thing worse than feeling inferior and that's being able to prove it.

—— ★ ——

I told the doctor I sometimes feel so inferior that I don't think anyone notices me at all. He said, "Next."

—— ★ ——

Because I feel inferior I try harder. Because I am inferior it doesn't do any good.

—— ★ ——

I have two basic problems. I think everyone else is better than me and so do they.

—— ★ ——

My doctor convinced me my inferiority complex was all in my mind, which he also convinced me is not as good as everybody else's.

—— ★ ——

The doctor told me he's seen inferiority complexes much worse than mine. Even my inferiority complex is inferior.

—— ★ ——

I had an inferiority complex even as a kid. I had an imaginary playmate who was ashamed to hang around with me.

—— ★ ——

I had an inferiority complex very early. At birth, when the doctor slapped my bottom I didn't cry. I felt I deserved it.

—— ★ ——

There are three kinds of lies—lies, damned lies, and statistics. —*Mark Twain*

There's one way to find out if a man is honest: ask him; if he says yes, you know he's crooked. —*Mark Twain*

If one tells the truth, one is sure, sooner or later, to be found out.
—*Oscar Wilde*

My wife never lies about her age. She just tells people she's as old as I am, then she lies about my age.
—*Milton Berle*

No man has a good enough memory to be a successful liar.
—*Abraham Lincoln*

George Washington said to his father: "If I never tell a lie, how can I get to be president?"
—*Red Buttons*

One of the most striking differences between a cat and a lie is that a cat has only nine lives.
—*Mark Twain*

My brother-in-law tells people he's a diamond cutter. He mows the lawn at Yankee Stadium.
—*Henny Youngman*

I told my wife the truth. I told her I was seeing a psychiatrist. Then she told me the truth: that she was seeing a psychiatrist, two plumbers, and a bartender.
—*Rodney Dangerfield*

Truth is something you leave in the locker room with your street shoes when you play golf.

Why is it when you tell a series of truths and a series of lies, people believe the lies?

The truth will never hurt you . . . unless you're talking to a new parent with a terribly unattractive child.

Anybody who says "Truth is stranger than fiction" has never read Stephen King.

When I tell a lie my palms get sweaty. When I tell the truth, the people I'm talking about get sweaty.

—— ★ ——

Pinocchio's nose got bigger every time he told an untruth. It kept him out of politics.

—— ★ ——

My mother always said "Tell the truth and shame the devil." I told the truth once and shamed my father.

—— ★ ——

My wife has been lying about her age for 15 years now. It started when she was 5 years younger.

—— ★ ——

Is wearing a toupee a lie? Or is it just a very funny looking near-truth?

—— ★ ——

Your lips may lie but your eyes will always tell the truth. This may give you a little insight into why Tonto never quite trusted the Lone Ranger.

—— ★ ——

Smart is when you believe only half of what you hear. Brilliant is when you know which half to believe.

—*Robert Orben*

In kindergarten, I flunked sandpile.

—*Joey Bishop*

You've got the brain of a four-year-old boy, and I bet he was glad to get rid of it.
—*Groucho Marx*

He's so intelligent. Talking with him is equivalent to passing the bar exam.

When I talk to him, I feel a dunce cap starting to grow out the top of my head.

This friend of mine has a good head on his shoulders. No neck, just a good head.

This guy is brilliant. He could explain Einstein's theory . . . to Einstein.

This guy uses words that are longer than my résumé.

I have a friend who is a flower child. He's a blooming idiot.

This guy took his dog to obedience school, and the dog got a higher grade than he did.

I asked this guy if he could think on his feet. He said, "Certainly. Who else's feet would I think on."

He not only thinks on his feet but apparently with them.

—— ★ ——

This guy is so dumb he thinks Shirley Temple is a synagogue for children.

—— ★ ——

Someone once explained to this guy that a comet was a star with a tail. He now thinks Lassie is a comet.

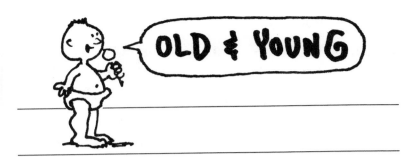

OLD & YOUNG

My husband was old. Ooooold. Older than his birthday.
—*Moms Mabley*

Middle-age is when work is a lot less fun, and fun is a lot more work. —*Milton Berle*

Life would be infinitely happier if we could only be born at the age of 80 and gradually approach 18.
—*Mark Twain*

An old man can't do nothin' for me except bring me a message from a young man. —*Moms Mabley*

He is so old his birth certificate is on a rock.
—*Jack Benny*

You're getting older when it takes you more time to recover than it did to tire you out. —*Milton Berle*

Anyone can get old. All you have to do is live long enough.
—*Groucho Marx*

Every morning when I get up, I read the obituary page. If my name's not there, I shave. —*George Burns*

There are certain signs when you're old. I walked past the cemetery the other day and two guys ran after me with shovels. —*Rodney Dangerfield*

Old age is when your liver spots show through your gloves.
—*Phyllis Diller*

He's so old, his blood type is discontinued.   —*Bill Dana*

I'll tell you how to keep looking young: hang around with older people.   —*Bob Hope*

He's so old that when he asks for a 3-minute egg, they ask for the money up front.   —*Milton Berle*

My husband said when he was young, he used to live in the country. I said, "When you were young, everybody lived in the country."   —*Moms Mabley*

You know you're old when everybody goes to your birthday party and stands around the cake just to get warm.   —*George Burns*

Remember that as a teenager you are at the last stage in your life when you will be happy to hear that the phone is for you.   —*Fran Lebowitz*

When you are eight years old, nothing is your business.   —*Lenny Bruce*

It's a good idea to have children while your parents are still young enough to take care of them.   —*Rita Rudner*

I'll never forget my youth. I was the teacher's pet. She couldn't afford a dog.   —*Rodney Dangerfield*

When I was young I had the cutest little button nose, but they couldn't feed me. It was buttoned to my lower lip.   —*Henny Youngman*

★   ★   ★   ★   ★

At my age, I refuse to wear a beeper. I don't want anything else on my body that might fall off.

Age gets to all of us sooner or later. It walks right up to you and says, "Do you know where I can find Dick Clark?"

He's so old, when he plays golf, he doesn't have to yell "Fore." His creaking bones warn the foursome ahead of him.

— ★ —

Youth can be a wonderful thing if you're young enough to enjoy it.

— ★ —

We knew they were too young to get married when they insisted on going to summer camp for their honeymoon.

— ★ —

Childish behavior: that's anyone who is doing what we only wish we could still do.

— ★ —

Middle-aged: that's what old people insist on calling themselves.

— ★ —

She couldn't wait to be old enough to get a face-lift so she could look younger.

— ★ —

He wore a toupee that made him look about ten years sillier.

— ★ —

Young people keep wanting to look older and old people keep wanting to look younger. Middle-aged people just keep looking for their reading glasses.

— ★ —

Old people just seem wiser because all they have to fool are the young people.

— ★ —

Middle-age is a time of life when the most fun you have is talking about the most fun you used to have.

— ★ —

They call it middle-age because it's the age at which your middle starts taking over.

— ★ —

He has no friends. He brought a parrot home and it told him to get out. —*Milton Berle*

I don't know what I'd do without you guys, but I'd rather. —*Frank Fay*

He hasn't an enemy in the world . . . but all his friends hate him. —*Jack E. Leonard*

She's so fat, she's my two best friends. —*Joan Rivers*

Always forgive your enemies.—Nothing annoys them so much. —*Oscar Wilde*

He's the kind of man who picks his friends—to pieces. —*Mae West*

The holy passion of friendship is of so sweet and steady and loyal and enduring a nature that it will last through a whole lifetime . . . if not asked to lend money. —*Mark Twain*

I like him. I have no taste, but I like him. —*Morey Amsterdam*

Harpo: She's her own worst enemy.
Groucho: Not while I'm alive she's not. —*Marx Brothers*

Fang and I are always fighting. When we get up in the morning, we don't kiss; we touch gloves. —*Phyllis Diller*

My best friend ran away with my wife, and let me tell you, I miss him. —*Henny Youngman*

Every time I look at you, I get a fierce desire to be lone-some. —*Oscar Levant*

I'm the kind of guy who will always be a friend to people in need. That's because people who are doing all right won't hang around with me.

I have a friend who is loyal, dependable, courageous, and strong. If he were only a St. Bernard, he'd be perfect.

I know a guy who will be my friend for life or until I pay him back the money I owe him, which is the same thing.

My best friend and I get along like brothers—Cain and Abel.

I have some friends who are just like money in the bank. You can only get to them during business hours.

I never turn my back on my friends. I don't trust them that much.

A friend is a guy who will lend you his last buck. An enemy is a guy who already did and now wants it back.

—— ★ ——

Think about it: If we didn't have enemies, how would we know who our friends are?

—— ★ ——

An enemy is sometimes nothing more than a friend who got wise to you. —— ★ ——

You show me a person who tells you to forgive your enemy, and I'll show you a person who will make a lousy divorce lawyer.

—— ★ ——

RICH & POOR

Those people were so rich they had a Persian rug made out of real Persians.
—*Henny Youngman*

My neighborhood was so poor, the only ailment anyone could afford was a fever. You starved that.
—*George Burns*

My family was so poor we couldn't give my sister a sweet-sixteen party until she was twenty-eight.   —*Joey Bishop*

When I was a kid, I was so poor I had to wear my brother's hand-me-downs—at the same time he was wearing them.
—*Redd Foxx*

I've been rich and I've been poor; rich is better.
—*Sophie Tucker*

Eleven kids in our family. We were so poor we had to wear each other's clothes. It wasn't funny. I had ten sisters.
—*Henny Youngman*

I came from a very poor family. They couldn't afford to have children; so our neighbor had me.
—*Henny Youngman*

We were so poor, at school I took algebra, history, and overcoats.
—*Jackie Vernon*

Rich? He takes cabs to drive-in movies.
—*Henny Youngman*

He's so rich he sends care packages to Nelson Rockefeller.
—*Bob Hope*

He's so rich his apartment has four area codes.
—*Jack E. Leonard*

Few of us can stand prosperity—another man's I mean.
—*Mark Twain*

★   ★   ★   ★   ★

I was very poor when I was a kid. My parents were wealthy, but I was poor.

—— ★ ——

We were so poor when I was kid all we had to wear were hand-me-downs, which was tough on me since I was an only child.

—— ★ ——

I never experienced poverty as a kid. My family couldn't afford it.

—— ★ ——

They say you can't take it with you. I never got to fool around with it much while I was here.

—— ★ ——

We never had much, but what we had wasn't ours.

—— ★ ——

You come into this life with nothing and you leave with nothing. It's a lot like asking a relative for a loan.

—— ★ ——

When you get right down to it, rich people are just poor people with money.

—— ★ ——

I gave my kids everything I never had as a child . . . and they laughed at them.

I have a friend who's a very rich undertaker. He drives a sports hearse.

I know a guy who's so rich if he ever goes broke, it'll take two trips.

Everything this guy touches turns to gold. That's why he can't eat finger foods.

This guy is so rich his butler has a chauffeur.

This guy is so rich he's got money he hasn't even had to lie about yet.

I know one guy who is so status-conscious that everything he does has got to be the richest. He even goes to a church with bucket pews.

It seems funny that all the people who hate the rich are the same ones who buy lottery tickets.

He might be considered a rich kid. His parents were so prominent they came from both sides of the tracks.

Beverly Hills is a very exclusive community. Costume jewelry here is considered a misdemeanor.

. . . In their telephone books, names aren't listed alphabetically. They're listed by net worth.

These kids were so rich their dad bought them a chauffeur-driven bicycle.

I'll give you an idea of how rich they are. If he ever tried to bury his money in the backyard, the East Coast would have a Grand Canyon, too.

He has the only wallet in the world that, in a pinch, can double as a wheelbarrow.

I don't know how he got all his money. Most people who have that much got it by declaring war against the United States and then losing.

Rich people go to prisons that are so plush the guards double as caddies.

They had a riot at one of those plush prisons a few years ago. Some innocent people were trying to break in.

Nobody knows how much he's worth. His money doesn't stay still long enough to be counted.

But as rich as he is, he uses his money for a good cause . . . to get more.

He's so rich he owns everything in town. If you put a quarter in a pay phone, his voice says, "Thank you."

Love. Everyone says looks don't matter. Age doesn't matter. Money doesn't matter, but I never met a girl yet who has fallen in love with an old, ugly man who's broke.
—*Rodney Dangerfield*

Love conquers all things except poverty and a toothache.
—*Mae West*

Love is staying awake all night with a sick child—or a healthy adult.
—*David Frost*

Love is like hash. You have to have confidence in it to enjoy it.
—*Bob Hope*

Everybody hates this guy. If he had a one-man show on Broadway he'd quit because he couldn't get along with the rest of the cast.
—*Bob Hope*

I hate smart salesclerks. I said to one, "What do you have in lingerie?" She said, "More than you'll ever have."
—*Phyllis Diller*

I am free of prejudice. I hate everyone equally.
—*W. C. Fields*

★　★　★　★　★

Love makes the world go 'round. It also makes many people wish it would stop so they could get off.

They say that love is blind and most of the people who sit on the bride's side of the church at a wedding tend to agree.

Love is insanity with a collaborator.

Birds do it and bees do it, which proves that winged creatures have no more sense than we have.

It's better to have loved a short person than never to have loved a tall.

Love is forever, so pack accordingly.

Love and hate are two sides of the same coin, although heads and tails are the more common terms.

Love can turn to hate. Divorce lawyers bank on it.

I would hate his guts if I thought he had any.

If there's anything I hate to death it's people who exaggerate.

This man has fun being wicked. He put the "ha" in hate.

There are two things I hate—hatred and people who divide everything into categories.

ACHES & PAINS

I told my doctor "It hurts when I do this." He said, "Don't do that."
—*Henny Youngman*

I'm not into working out. My philosophy: no pain, no pain
—*Carol Leifer*

I went up to visit the doctor with my sore foot. He said, "I'll have you walking in an hour." He did. He stole my car.
—*Henny Youngman*

When I was young, if any of us kids got sick, my mother would bring out the chicken soup. Of course, that didn't work for broken bones. For broken bones she gave boiled beef.
—*George Burns*

My doctor said, "Have you ever had this pain before?" I said, "Yes." He said, "You've got it again."
—*Henny Youngman*

I asked my doctor what to do for a sprained ankle. He said, "Limp."
—*Milton Berle*

★ ★ ★ ★ ★

I have so many aches and pains that I list liniment as one of my hobbies.

—— ★ ——

The only parts of my body that don't hurt are parts that don't work anymore.

109

When I get out of bed in the morning the only thing on me that doesn't hurt is my pajamas.

I have so many aches and pains. If it weren't for Ace bandages, I'd have no wardrobe at all.

I had a muscle that twitched all day yesterday. It's the most exercise I've had in years.

The other day my foot fell asleep. The embarrassing part was that it snored.

I had tennis elbow for so long I finally had to take up the game.

I had some strange ailment where I broke out in little dots all over my body. I asked my doctor what I should do. He said, "Don't wear plaid."

I told my doctor I couldn't lift my hands above my head. He told me to stay away from muggers.

I told my doctor I wanted to do some travelling, but I had all these aches and pains. He taught me how to say "ow" in six different languages.

My mommy used to use kisses to make my hurts go away. My doctor says he'll stick with aspirin.

I have such poor vision, I could date anyone.
—*Garry Shandling*

I'm so nearsighted, I can't even see my contact lenses.
—*Henny Youngman*

The only reason I wear glasses is for little things—like driving my car—or finding it.   —*Woody Allen*

How are your eyes, mama? You still see spots in front of them? Put on your glasses. How is it now? You see the spots much clearer.   —*George Jessel*

This woman is so cross-eyed, she can go to a tennis match and never move her head.   —*Phyllis Diller*

I have poor eyesight. When I take an eye test, the doctor points to the letters and he calls them out and says, "True or false?"   —*Woody Allen*

★   ★   ★   ★   ★

Nature's wonderful. The older looking you get, the harder it is to see yourself in the mirror.

—— ★ ——

You know you've reached middle-age when everything in the contract is in small print.

—— ★ ——

What scares me is all those people who can't read the menu in restaurants are going to be in their cars driving home at the same time I am.

My eyes are so bad, I can't read menus anymore. I have to order from the pictures on the menu. One time I ordered the front of the restaurant.

My dad would never admit his eyes were failing. He'd say, "Son, I can look you right in the face and tell you that my eyesight is as good as ever." I'd have to say, "Pop. I'm over here."

——— ★ ———

Everything goes when you get older. I asked my grandfather if he'd like me to read the paper to him. He said, "What?"

——— ★ ———

My grandfather was an excellent marksman well into his 80's. His only problem was he couldn't read the "No Hunting" signs.

——— ★ ———

Everything goes when you get older. I can't read newspaper print anymore. I can still see the pictures, but I can't remember who the people are.

Failing eyesight is Mother Nature's way of slowing us down as we grow older. "Why should you spend so much time reading today," she says, "when you won't remember most of it tomorrow anyway?"

I don't understand Mother Nature. How come when we get older our eyes start to fail but we can still smell as good as ever?

——— ★ ———

My eyes were so bloodshot one time I could watch a lovely sunset at noon.

——— ★ ———

FORGETFUL

There are three signs of old age: loss of memory ... I forget the other two.
—*Red Skelton*

Nothing is more responsible for the good old days than a bad memory.
—*Robert Benchley*

Am I forgetful? Last night I forgot the Alamo.
—*Henny Youngman*

When I was younger I could remember anything, whether it happened or not. But I am getting old and soon I shall remember only the latter.
—*Mark Twain*

The short memories of the American voters is what keeps our politicians in office.
—*Will Rogers*

I have a poor memory for names, but I never remember a face.
—*W. C. Fields*

★　★　★　★　★

My memory is starting to go. I locked the keys in my car the other day. Fortunately, I had forgotten to get out first.

The memory is not the first thing to go. It's just that when it goes, you forget about all the other things that went before it.

—— ★ ——

I've forgotten more about memory loss than you'll ever know.

There are some good things about having a bad memory. Like last week I threw myself a surprise party.

. . . Then I forgot to go.

I have trouble remembering faces. I left mine at home four times last week.

When I got home my wife said, "Did you remember to get milk? Did you pick up the dry cleaning? Did you get the car washed?" I not only forgot those things; I forgot I was married.

There's a strange thing about memory. Damned if I can remember what it is.

I can remember things from years ago, but I can't remember what I had for breakfast this morning. Wait a minute! I forgot to have breakfast this morning.

I went to see a new doctor. He said, "That'll be $25 in advance." I paid him and told him I had a terrible short-term memory. He said, "That'll be $25 in advance."

My doctor prescribed pills for my memory. I'm supposed to take one three times a day if I can remember where they are.

My brother's memory is just as bad as mine. We both think we're an only child.

"It's easier to love humanity as a whole than to love one's neighbor."
—*Eric Hoffer*

I quit smoking. I feel better, I smell better, and it's safer to drink from old beer cans around the house.

—*Roseanne Barr*

People are so rude to smokers. You'd think they'd try to be nicer to people that are dying. —*Roseanne Barr*

I smoke cigars because at my age if I don't have something to hang onto I might fall down. —*George Burns*

I know it's very easy to give up smoking because I've tried it so often. —*Mark Twain*

I never smoke to excess—that is, I smoke in moderation, only one cigar at a time. —*Mark Twain*

* * * * *

A lot of people are getting very militant against smokers. The warning on the pack now says, "Smoking may be injurious to your health. The person sitting next to you may hit you with a stick."

—— ★ ——

You heard of "Where there's smoke there's fire?" That's been changed to "Where there's smoke there's someone nearby making a face and calling you a dirty name."

—— ★ ——

They don't allow smoking in most restaurants now. In fact, some even frown on customers ordering anything well done.

—— ★ ——

Restaurants have smaller and smaller smoking sections now. I know one where smoking is only allowed in the kitchen oven that's not being used.

Los Angeles restaurants are getting very strict against smoking. They have a smoking section but it's in Oxnard.

All domestic air flights are nonsmoking now. The most fun smokers can have on airplanes now is turning down the food.

The only way you can smoke on a domestic flight nowadays is to be one of the engines.

Some smokers are trying to get around the regulation by disguising themselves as luggage.

They figure it's worth the risk of getting lost.

If you're on a long flight and you absolutely have to smoke, you can always step outside.

. . . It's a long first step, but for some smokers it's worth it.

Smokers on airplanes are now getting desperate. I saw a guy on one flight who was trying to inhale the little picture of a cigarette on the "No Smoking" sign.

On long flights now, if an engine starts smoking the passengers don't get mad. They get jealous.

They may have to have two masks available on the planes from now on—one filled with oxygen, the other filled with nicotine.

One day my wife drove up the side of a building . . . and hit another woman driving down.   *—Milton Berle*

I bought my wife a new car. Three weeks ago she learned how to drive it. Last week she learned how to aim it.
   —Henny Youngman

I sometimes have trouble starting my car. The ignition keeps spitting out the key.   *—Phyllis Diller*

Who would give me a driver's license? I got two tickets on my written test.   *—Phyllis Diller*

Whenever I rent a car, in order to cut down on the mileage rate, I back up everywhere.   *—Woody Allen*

A wife told her husband, "Be an angel and let me drive." He did and he is.   *—Milton Berle*

★   ★   ★   ★   ★

Some people treat driving as a means of transportation. Others consider it a contact sport.

It may be the fault of the car manufacturers. Too many drivers take the term *bumpers* literally.

—— ★ ——

Driving today is America's last surviving form of guerrilla warfare.

The way some people drive, it seems they should put on war paint before turning on the ignition.

Many people drive simply to get where they're going; others for revenge.

We should have stayed with horseback as the predominant means of transportation. At least with horses we didn't have to put up with obnoxious bumper stickers.

It seems today that road courtesy went out with running boards.

We all hate aggressive drivers. They're the ones who try to get back at us after we cut them off.

I know one driver who gets on the road and immediately pulls into the fast lane . . . whether there's another car there already or not.

The way some people drive, their car is not considered an automobile. It's considered an accomplice.

I have one friend who speeds constantly. His one goal in life is to never have another car in front of him.

You know you're getting too angry behind the wheel when you can light up without using the car's cigarette lighter.

I have a large seashell collection which I keep scattered along the beaches around the world. Maybe you've seen it.
—*Steven Wright*

Why does the ocean roar? You'd roar too if you had that many crabs on your bottom. —*Redd Foxx*

What about all those detergents that are going out to our rivers and oceans? If this keeps up, it's going to leave a ring around the country. —*John Byner*

Our waters are so dirty. Many of our fishes are beaching themselves and asking for asylum. —*Bob Hope*

Our waters are in trouble. The other day a dam gave way, but the lake didn't. —*Milton Berle*

★   ★   ★   ★   ★

The sea has a soothing effect. Have you ever seen a nervous clam?

Two-thirds of the earth's surface is covered with water. That's a lot like my basement when I tried to do my own plumbing.

—— ★ ——

Some of our fish now have so much mercury in them, they can take their own temperature.

—— ★ ——

Our oceans are so dirty they have signs at some beaches that read, "Please wipe your feet before leaving the ocean."

You know our waters are getting pretty dirty. Fish have begun washing their food before eating it.

There are so many oil slicks in the oceans now that every time the tide comes in, it slips right out again.

Twice a year all the oceans have to be brought in now for an oil change.

I've heard of tuna packed in oil, but not while they were still swimming around.

When an octopus puts on deodorant, how does he remember where he started?

Fish is supposed to be brain food. How much brain does it take to bite into a plastic worm with a hook in it?

I'm not a fish eater. The only seafood I'll eat is salt-water taffy.

. . . unless it has bones in it.

COMING SOON...

HEAVEN & HELL

"I do benefits for all religions. I'd
hate to go to hell on a technicality."
—*Bob Hope*

Eternal rest sounds comforting in the pulpit. Well, you try it once and see how heavy time will hang on your hands.
—*Mark Twain*

When asked to join a discussion of eternal life and future punishment, Mark Twain replied, "I am silent of necessity; I have friends in both places."   —*Mark Twain*

★   ★   ★   ★   ★

You have to be really good to go to heaven. Years ago my parents told me the same thing about Disneyland.

—— ★ ——

Heaven is very important to my mom. She's always wanted to live in a gated community.

—— ★ ——

You have to die to go to heaven. It's kind of the ultimate retirement village.   —— ★ ——

I'm worried about going to heaven. When St. Peter opens up the Pearly Gates, what do you tip him?

—— ★ ——

Wouldn't it be terrible to get to heaven and see a sign posted on the Pearly Gates that reads, "This Property Protected by the Ajax Alarm System"?

—— ★ ——

Only good people go to heaven. So the *National Enquirer* up there makes for very dull reading.

What do you do if you want to go to heaven, but you hate harp music?

I have this fear that when I get to heaven, God's going to hand me a set of angel wings, and I'm going to have to tell Him I'm afraid of heights.

—— ★ ——

One guy got to heaven and became an angel. He said, "Now you give me the wings. I died in a bungee-jumping accident."

—— ★ ——

There is one bad feature of going to heaven—anything you bought on a lifetime guarantee is no longer covered.

—— ★ ——

Heaven is forever. So bring plenty of reading material.

—— ★ ——

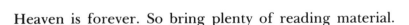

A diplomat is a person who can tell you to go to hell in such a way that you actually look forward to the trip.
—*Caskie Stinnett*

My wife converted me to religion. I never believed in hell until I married her. —*Hal Roach*

People in hell—where do they tell people to go? —*Red Skelton*

★　★　★　★　★

It's possible that hell could just be heaven without room service.

——— ★ ———

Hell is forever . . . it just seems longer.

——— ★ ———

Hell is one place where losers can never say "Wait 'til next year."

——— ★ ———

Heaven is for good people. Hell is for those who don't want to spend eternity hanging around with good people.

——— ★ ———

I wonder if hell has a smoking and nonsmoking section.

——— ★ ———

He's the kind of egotist who could go through hell with a "holier than thou" attitude.

——— ★ ———

Hell is a place full of fire and brimstone—kind of like Los Angeles during the dry season.

——— ★ ———

That might be one of the easiest jobs of all time—being a bouncer in hell.

——— ★ ———

Wouldn't it be ironic if on the gates of hell there was a sign posted that read "We reserve the right to refuse admittance to anyone"?

——— ★ ———

I don't want to be sent to hell, but with the luck I've been having with my travel agent lately . . .

—— ★ ——

Hell is supposed to be a bad place, but you can't believe that because everyone who goes there is a liar.

—— ★ ——

I happen to be the suspicious type. For instance, I've always felt that reincarnation is just a sneaky way to sell more tombstones. *—Robert Orben*

If I believed in reincarnation, I'd come back as a sponge. *—Woody Allen*

I believe in reincarnation. I've had other lives. I know. I've had clues. First of all, I'm exhausted. *—Carol Siskind*

In the next life, I'd like to come back as an oyster. Then I'd only have to be good from September to April. *—Gracie Allen*

There's nothing wrong with you that reincarnation won't cure. *—Jack E. Leonard*

★ ★ ★ ★ ★

Reincarnation may be nature's way of saying, "Okay, let's make it best two out of three."

—— ★ ——

If I'm going to come back to life, why am I dieting so much to keep this one in shape?

I like the idea of reincarnation. Toys today are so much more fun than they were when I was a kid.

I don't know if I've ever lived before. I can't remember half the things I've done in this life.

I don't like the thought of reincarnation. It's discouraging to think that I may have lived ten or twelve lives before this, and I still don't know how to hit a golf ball.

If there is such a thing as reincarnation, then death isn't really death. It's just a chance to get a quick shower and a change of clothes.

——— ★ ———

Just on the outside chance that there is reincarnation, I'm leaving everything in my will to me . . . whoever I may be at the time.

——— ★ ———

I'll go along with reincarnation with one reservation: I don't want to come back in the next life at an entry-level position.

——— ★ ———

There could just be such a thing as reincarnation. So don't make fun of your great-grandfather. He just might be you.

——— ★ ———

You die, you come back. You die, you come back. You die, you come back. It's a terrible way to go through eternity . . . as a yo-yo.

——— ★ ———

INDEX